I0440799

Be Set Free Fast

Training Manual

*How To Use Energy Therapy
To Eliminate Anxieties And
Create A Happy Fulfilling Life*

*By Rosemary Harper, MSW ***

*Be Set Free Fast is a registered Trade mark
of Larry Phillip Nims, Ph D. Clinical Psychologist
1400 East Chapman Ave. Orange, California

What This Method Can Do For You:

Any problem that you might have, or any self-improvement goal that you might set, can be dramatically aided by the correct application of this version of energy therapy.

This means virtually any problem you can think of that has a psychological basis, either in whole or in part. For example, in the area of medical problems, high blood pressure may be caused purely by a medical condition, or it may be the result of stress or other psychological factors. That component of the problem that is essentially non-medical can be treated quickly, easily and effectively by the proper application of the technique which you are about to learn here.

This is not about alternative medicine. If you have a medical problem, by all means see your doctor. Yet it is an undeniable fact that many human ailments are caused, or aggravated by, such things as stress, trauma, or negative mental programming.

An example might be an anxious person who heads for the fridge whenever they feel stressed. Eating might make them feel good for the time being, but can lead to obesity, which in turn can trigger a whole host of ailments, such as high blood pressure and diabetes. Now you do have a medical problem. Yet it has emotional roots. Clear those up through using this therapy method, and you may not need the doctor anymore.

It is not necessary to know that a problem has these emotional roots, either, or to what extent they may lie behind the issue at hand. You simply use this therapy as though it does have emotional roots. If such was the case, the problem will be dealt with- if not, no harm is done. All you stand to lose is the problem.

Any form of anxiety can be dealt with very effectively through use of this method. Do you get nervous when called upon to stand up and speak before a group? This is easily dealt with. Any phobias, such as fear of crowds, or flying, are treated just as easily.

Perhaps you would simply like to have lots more money. How do you know that your subconscious mind is not holding you back? (If you have a gambling problem, it certainly is). Find out, quickly and easily. Then treat for it.

Problems in personal relationships a concern? Help clear them up (at least on your side of things!) by the application of this technique.

Maybe you would simply like to lower your golf handicap? It is no secret that an important part of any sports performance is the mental side of the game, as witness the growth in the sports psychologist field. Sharpen up your game by using these techniques.

In the business world, it is going to be very difficult to get ahead if some elements of your subconscious programming are holding you back. Get them on-side by making sure your subconscious mind is working for you, not against you!

Why settle for anything less than achieving your full potential? The key to a happy, rewarding life is to harness the tremendous abilities of the subconscious mind. The technique you are about to learn is designed to do exactly that.

Your Subconscious Mind:

From the moment you are born, the subconscious mind starts processing data. Everything that happens to you, whether good or bad, is analysed and stored away. Our attitudes toward life in general, how we view those around us, the way we react to either stress or opportunity- all these things and more are a product of the way our subconscious mind is programmed.

There are two important concepts here. First, the subconscious mind is an extremely powerful force. Second, it is not easily influenced by the day to day thought processes of the conscious mind. All the usual daily trivia we are subject to is scrutinised by the subconscious mind, but if it is not judged significant, it is stored away somewhere in our mental basement.

This filtering out of "mental noise" is essential to keep us from being bogged down in irrelevant detail. It also makes it difficult for the conscious mind to get a message through to the more powerful mind below.

The subconscious mind is continually making value judgements as to what is, or is not, important. It does this in accordance with the dictates of its programming. This programming is not something that is easily influenced by stray thoughts from above.

We may say, for example, that we wish to be successful. But the subconscious mind may hold a different view of our real motives, based on our past reactions and attitudes. Until we can convince the subconscious mind otherwise, it may continue to be programmed for failure.

For the subconscious mind is capable of delivering almost any outcome. If we have inadvertently told it we want to fail, it will ensure that we do.

On the other hand, if it is programmed for success, then it can literally move mountains to bring this about. Clearly then, if we can find a method which will reach down and reprogram a dysfunctional command set, then our own subconscious mind becomes the most powerful ally we can have.

The Difficulties of Conventional Therapy:

Psychoanalysis is a therapy method founded by Sigmund Freud, and other psychiatrists developed variations of his technique. Basically, psychoanalysts believe that unpleasant experiences, especially during childhood, may become buried in the subconscious mind and cause problems. Treatment consists of trying to bring these experiences out of a patient's subconscious mind and into the conscious mind.

The problem is, this approach requires a long dialog between patient and therapist. This usually means three to five sessions a week and typically lasts for two to five years. Thus, ferreting out the offending material from the subconscious mind is a long, difficult, and very expensive process. Even then, understanding the cause of the problem is not necessarily the same as curing it.

Conventional psychiatry uses a number of treatments for mental disorders. Somatic therapy usually involves the use of medications, such as antidepressants, while psychotherapy is based on discussions between the patient and the psychiatrist.

Again, this may mean sessions once or twice a week for several months. Behaviour therapy uses rewards and punishments to encourage patients to change their behaviour, rather than trying to help them understand why they act the way they do.

All these methods have their place when dealing with mental health problems, but are clearly not suited to more casual use, or as part of any self-help regime because they are invasive, time-consuming and expensive. Someone suffering from schizophrenia needs such professional care, but most would balk at the money and commitment required when all they want to do is fix a public speaking phobia or lower their golf score! What is needed, then, is a simple and efficient method of tapping into the subconscious mind. This is where energy therapy comes into the picture.

A Short History of Energy Therapy:

Energy therapy is a general term for treatments which claim that a perturbation in the energy field of the person involved causes some problem, and that this problem can be treated by tapping on specific energy circuits to bring the energy system into balance. This is a sort of "psychic acupuncture" if you like. In this simple form, energy therapy does not address any subconscious programming, or get at the root causes of problems.

About 17 years ago, a psychologist in the USA, Dr. Roger Callahan, developed an effective treatment for phobias. These "Callahan Techniques", which are now called Thought Field Therapy, (TFT) aimed to alleviate the problems caused by negative emotions. The key was the concept that these emotional problems are controlled by the electromagnetic fields that are operating continuously within our bodies. Influence that field and you can influence the problem.

The Callahan Techniques, although effective, form a complex and elaborate system of diagnosing and treating psychological problems, and are designed for use by trained professionals.

In 1990, Dr. Larry Phillip Nims, a Clinical Psychologist, was among the first few professionals trained by Dr. Callahan in his techniques. Over the years, Dr. Nims developed his own method, which he calls BSFF, or Be Set Free Fast. The full name of this therapy is: behavioral & emotional symptom elimination training for resolving excess emotion- fear, anger, sadness and trauma.

Dr. Nims' BSFF technique, which is the method you are about to learn in this manual, while being an outgrowth of Dr. Callahan's techniques, involves a quite different theoretical understanding of the source of psychological problems. This different focus has resulted in a treatment which gets the same results but is simpler, faster, and easier to learn. This means that for the first time, there is a technique which may be safely used by other than trained psychologists.

Within Australia, Mr. Don Heggie has sponsored a series of seminars by Dr. Nims, to teach his method to health care professionals in our country. In collaboration with Don Heggie and Dr. Nims, we propose to bring this invaluable method to a wider audience, by making this manual available to help anyone who wishes to learn the techniques.

Some Facts About Emotional Problems:

The subconscious mind carries a complete and detailed record of everything that has ever happened to us. Negative experiences in our past can lock in strong negative emotions, and result in a subconscious mind that is programmed not for success, but for failure.

Through the adoption of incorrect belief systems (which are the deepest causes), our subconscious mind is quite capable of sabotaging our course through life.

Professionals call this a Psychological Reversal, and it results in our wanting one thing, but doing another, which leads to failure. The good news is, when this negative programming is reversed, the subconscious mind becomes the most powerful ally we can have.

Rooting out problems can be difficult. A particular problem may have something like 700 to 2,000 emotional roots behind it. These stem from a multitude of past experiences involving sadness, fear, trauma or anger, which are associated with the particular problem.

It can be readily seen that conventional therapies that seek to identify all of these root causes to problems face a time-consuming uphill battle. The beauty of the BSFF method is that all these root causes can be eliminated at a stroke, without delving into them on an individual basis.

So each individual problem has its own set of emotional roots, and every problem limits us in some specific way. This may show up in the form of difficulties with our relationships, our financial dealings, occupation, or our social attitudes and self-image. Because it is difficult to see our own flaws and limitations, it is often hard to realise we have a problem in the first place.

Again, treatment to clear a particular problem may not succeed, because some other problem needs to be treated first. Finding and identifying problems then, may require professional help or guidance. This is why consultation with a trained professional is offered as a supplement to this manual.

BSFF Explained:

What then does the technique entail? Once a problem has been identified, basically, it consists of tapping on certain treatment spots, while repeating statements relating to the problem. This is done in conjunction with a procedure called muscle testing, which is used to provide feedback on how the treatment is progressing.

The Treatment Points:

Treatment spot #1　This is the focal point for an electromagnetic circuit associated with sadness and trauma. It is located on the inner ridge of either eye socket, just above the nose. See photo number 1.

Photo # 1

Hurt
Dismay
Disappointment
Discouraged
Hopeless
Rejected
Grief
Lonely

Treat here for sadness and trauma:

Treatment spot #2 is the tapping point used for fears and anxiety of any sort. This point is located about a half-inch below the bottom center of either eye socket, as depicted in photo number 2.

Photo # 2

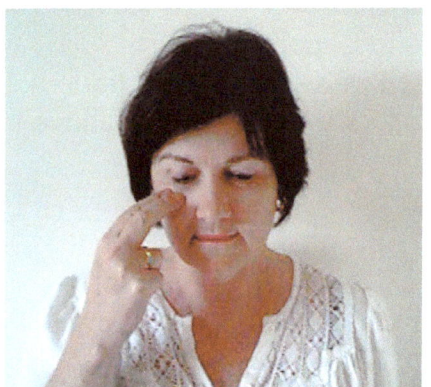

Anxious
Nervous
Tense
Hesitant
Phobias
Obsessive
Worry
Shy
Pressured

Treat here for fear and anxiety:

Treatment spot #3   Problems relating to anger, resentment or irritation are dealt with by tapping on the inside (nearest the thumb) of the little finger, just behind the nail. This is shown in photo number 3.

Photo # 3

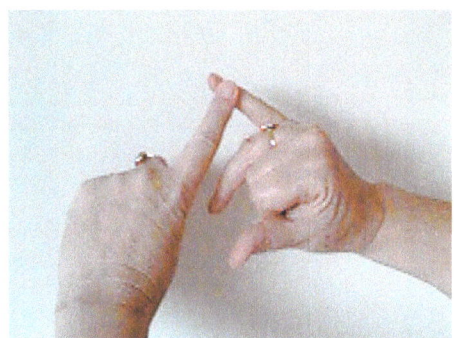

Treat here for anger:

Mad
Frustrated
Rage
Resentment
Outraged
Irritated
Aggravated

Treatment spot #4   Eliminating all issues of unforgiveness (including anger with yourself) is handled by tapping beside the fingernail of the first finger, on the side nearest the thumb. Photo number 4 illustrates this procedure.

Photo # 4   **Treat here for forgiveness:**

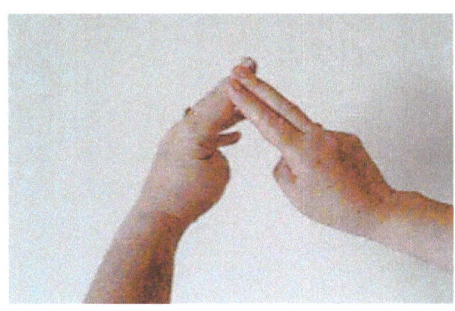

"I forgive...

..myself
..society
..God
..Sally, Robert, etc.

The Procedure:

The first step in any BSFF session is to think of the problem you wish to eliminate. This may be done in general terms, and need not be detailed. The purpose is simply to bring the problem to the forefront of your conscious mind. While keeping this problem in mind, begin by treating for *sadness.*

1. This is done by tapping gently on **treatment spot #1** while saying the following statement once only: *"I am eliminating all of the sadness in all of the roots- and the deepest cause- of all of this problem."*

2. Next, any possible fear component of the problem is dealt with by tapping on **treatment spot #2** while repeating *" I am eliminating all of the fear in all of the roots- and the deepest cause- of all of this problem."*

3. When that is done, move on to treat any anger associated with the problem. This is done by tapping on **treatment spot #3** in conjunction with the sentence *"I am eliminating all of the anger in all of the roots- and the deepest cause- of all of this problem."*

4. Treat for problems related to emotional trauma by once again tapping on **treatment spot #1**, only this time the focus is on trauma, and the sentence used is: *"I am eliminating all of the emotional trauma in all of the roots- and the deepest cause- of all of this problem."*

5. Finally, use **treatment spot #4**, to deal with issues of unforgiveness. You are very likely to be angry at yourself for having the problem in the first place, and many problems are bound up with anger towards others, including (if you are

religious) God, or society in general, so it is crucial to go through this step. While each of the previous four steps involved saying or thinking the relevant sentence once only, the procedure for forgiveness is a little different. While tapping continuously on the index finger as shown in photo #4, the sentence concerned is repeated **three times.**

Also, forgiveness issues (and anger) should be dealt with on an individual basis, rather than employing a blanket statement. Some examples follow:

"I forgive myself, and I know that I did the best I could."

"I forgive you (Mom, Dad, Jim, Sally, etc.) and I know that you were doing the best you could."

"I forgive you, Lord, and I know you are always here and doing the right thing for me."

These are just examples, and may be modified into something you feel comfortable with. Note though, that you are not saying these statements to convince yourself or anyone else. It is not necessary for you to believe these statements- they will still work!

The Anger-Forgiveness Connection:

Note that in step 3, while treating for anger, a generic statement is made in the form of: *"I am eliminating all of the anger in all of the roots- and the deepest cause- of all of this problem."* This is fine for a starting point, but, in addition, issues of anger and forgiveness should be dealt with on an individual basis, as they are identified.

Since it is quite rare for anyone not to be mad at themselves concerning problems, the safe thing to do is to treat as though anger at self is present, and treat for it specifically in step 3, then treat for forgiveness of self in step 5. This sequence should be repeated for any other identified sources of anger.

Always save the treatment for anger and forgiveness towards self for the very last treatment in any given session of BSFF. It doesn't make sense to treat self-anger before all other angers and forgiveness issues are treated.

The goal is to resolve all anger issues towards others first, then treat for the problem of being angry at others. Adhering to this order will prevent unresolved anger issues from being left behind.

It is important to deal with anger issues before attempting forgiveness, since anger sways judgement and distorts the way we see things. Until the anger is acknowledged and dealt with, forgiveness is difficult, because clouded or biased opinions will simply re-create the hostility. Some people get a sort of perverse satisfaction from their anger, yet if they keep the anger, they also keep the problem. Deal with it. Treat for anger, then forgiveness, and the problem ends.

This is the basic procedure, which is used to deal with problems of any sort. Sadness, fear, anger, and trauma are dealt with in that order. Note that no value judgements are made to try to decide which of these emotional factors are behind the problem at hand, or to what extent they may be present. You simply treat as though they are all present, and by doing so, take no chances of leaving any part of the problem untouched.

It should also be noted that the sentences used do not constitute a magical incantation: they are simply designed to "key" the proper thoughts into the subconscious mind, and to overlook nothing. Any similar phraseology would do the job. Also, they may be said out loud, or simply be repeated mentally. They get to the subconscious either way. To understand why these key sentences are structured the way they are, it is helpful to give a bit more detail about what emotional roots and deepest causes mean.

Emotional Roots:

The emotional roots which contribute to any given problem are simply those events or impressions which have left a negative impact upon us in some area or another. These roots may have been piling up right from early childhood days, so there could be lots of them. Although the actual events which triggered them may have been forgotten or suppressed by the conscious mind, they are all carefully catalogued and stored away within the subconscious.

They impact on us most often in the form of feelings of fear, anger or sadness. These unresolved experiences get locked into electromagnetic circuits and result in the adoption of inappropriate belief systems which in turn result in negative behaviour patterns. BSFF helps to empty these electronic trash bins and allow a fresh start. If you're a computer buff, this is just like emptying the recycle bin in Windows.

Deepest Cause:

Simply put, the deepest cause is the basic belief which underlies the problem. In other words, the emotional roots may have caused a person to look at the world in a certain negative way. Once these emotional roots have been neutralised, it is then necessary to sweep away the resulting inappropriate belief set as well, so a new, more positive belief can replace it. Thus, when we say *"I am eliminating all of the anger in all of the roots- and the deepest cause- of all of this problem."* we ensure that the subconscious gets the message that both the roots and the deepest cause must be dealt with, and the "all" part of the statement ensures that nothing gets left behind.

Related Problems:

After this five step procedure has been done, you should check yourself to see if you still feel any distress. If you do, it means that you have another related problem which must be dealt with. The five BSFF steps are repeated, only this time you say *"I'm now treating this next problem."* The same pattern is repeated for each successive problem until you feel relaxed and at peace within.

Subjective Units Of Distress:

A simple way to gauge how you feel about any problem is to rate your distress on a scale from one to ten, with ten being the maximum anxiety. If you do this before initiating treatment, it provides a yardstick to test your progress, as each successive problem is dealt with. It is a good idea to write down this starting figure to get an accurate assessment later.

Psychologists use this method to quantify the impact of stress or emotional impact, using the term "subjective units of distress" (SUD). It is of course, the person being treated who must make the judgement, since only they are in a position to know how strongly they feel about a problem.

It can be seen that once a problem has been identified, and brought to the attention of the conscious mind, the BSFF treatment to eliminate this problem is relatively simple and quick. The skill lies in identifying the problem and bringing it forth so it may be treated. First of all, what is a problem?

Dr. Nims defines a "problem" as any automatic reaction which limits us in some way. This limitation may be mental, emotional, physical, spiritual, occupational, financial, domestic or social. Any of these limitations which holds us back from reaching our full potential constitutes a problem which should be treated using BSFF.

Each individual problem will have its own set of emotional roots and a deepest cause, and will require separate treatment. This is not the daunting task it may appear to be, because the BSFF technique is so fast. While there may be a multitude of interrelated problems, most people will find little difficulty knowing where to start.

Just like cleaning an untidy basement, the thing to do is to tackle the most obvious chore first. Once that is done, other problems will become more noticeable. For example, only when our floor is swept clean, will we be able to see the cracks and flaws which may need attention. So it is with our mental basement. Each change in a "deepest cause" or a belief set, will bring new insights, which in turn will shed fresh light on perhaps hitherto unrealised problems.

The Role Of Muscle Testing:

Muscle testing can be used as a stand-alone method which provides instant knowledge about what is going on in the subconscious mind, and so may also be used to identify problems. This technique grew out of a field of study called Applied Kinesiology. Although muscle testing has been around for perhaps hundreds of years, it is only in the past 40 to 50 years that it has become widely used. What it does, when used with the BSFF procedure, is provide a sort of instant biofeedback, so that progress can be quickly checked.

Basically, muscles are activated by tiny electrical impulses originating in the brain. In the normal course of events, if we wish to pick up a pencil, for example, this thought is first formed in the brain, and then the necessary electrical stimulus is sent out to the appropriate muscle groups, which turn the thought into reality.

When we make an assertion relating to a psychological problem, the subconscious mind will know whether that statement is correct or incorrect, and this "yes" or "no" response will vary the electrical signals sent out to the body's various muscle groups.

An acupuncturist would explain this in terms of "meridians" or specific electromagnetic circuits in the body. Each of the 14 meridians are said to have a parallel circuit on each side of the body, and each of these meridians influences a specific organ system in the body. BSFF theory assumes at least some of these circuits act as a locking mechanism binding together a specific combination of unresolved emotions and the associated belief system.

Whatever the explanation, the key point which makes muscle testing so useful is the very real observation that a statement which the subconscious mind tests as "true" will cause muscles to strengthen, or "lock" in place. Any statement the subconscious mind regards as "false" will have the reverse effect, and the muscle weakens. Thus, if we test a muscle group while repeating the relevant statement, the body's reaction provides a direct window into how the subconscious has been programmed. It acts as a sort of "lie detector" test.

How To Muscle Test Someone:

One of the easiest ways to muscle test a person is to have them extend either arm straight outward with the palm down. Ask them to hold the arm firm, and lock the muscles in place, while you exert downward pressure on the arm. This is done by placing your hand firmly on top of their wrist and pressing down on their arm until it starts to bend. A downward movement of two or three inches is all it takes to confirm that the arm is no longer locked.

Next, lighten the pressure just enough so that their arm no longer moves downward. The intent here is to determine the pressure differential required to overcome the locked position of the arm. This will obviously vary if either party regards this as a test of strength, which is not the purpose.

The tester is merely trying to establish the normal pressure required to overcome a "locked position" and the person being tested does not want to tire themselves. Should they get fatigued during any session, they may use the other arm- it won't affect the test results, since the muscle locking phenomena applies to all muscle groups.

Now, while exerting the pressure just at that differential point, have the subject make a statement that is entirely correct. Test to ensure the arm is still locked. Then have the subject make a statement which is clearly incompatible or opposite, while again exerting downward pressure. If the arm unlocks and moves down, this signals an incorrect statement.

When testing, it is important that the statements be unambiguous. An easy starting point with someone called George might be: "My name is George", followed by "my name is Harry". The first statement should test strong, while the second one should be weak.

When the arm muscle is strong, or locks, it means that the person's subconscious mind considers the statement to be 100% correct. If the muscle unlocks, or is weak, then the subconscious mind is signalling that the statement is less than 100% correct, though it might still be partially correct.

Muscle testing provides a window to see into the subconscious mind, and the opinions expressed there are not necessarily the ones anticipated by either the tester or the subject. When such a situation arises, it can provide valuable insights into potential problems.

This strong-weak reaction can also be observed in general human interactions, when no question at all is posed. Simply thinking about something pleasant will yield a positive response while an unpleasant thought will trigger a negative or weak result. Someone smiling at you will cause a positive signal, while a frown will trigger the reverse- an interesting insight into the way humans interact with each other.

How To Test Yourself:

It is possible to test yourself, should that be more convenient. Because muscle testing is a skill, any attempt at self-testing is best left until the practitioner feels reasonably comfortable with the conventional arm testing method, and is happy with its validity and reliability. Dr. Nims doesn't introduce clients to self-testing until they have experienced routine muscle testing about 50 to 100 times.

There are many ways to do the self-test. One of the simplest is to extend the index, or pointer finger, and hold it firmly by locking the muscles in place. Now place the middle finger on top of the index finger and press down until the index finger just starts to bend, then reduce the pressure until it no longer bends at all.

The idea is to find the differential point where just a bit more pressure would cause the index finger to bend. Using this amount of pressure, the index finger should move down when a test statement is not 100% correct, and remain locked when the statement is entirely correct.

If it feels more convenient, or comfortable, you can use the index finger of the opposite hand to press down on the index finger being tested. Or the thumb and middle finger of one hand can be brought together to form an "O" while the index finger of the other hand is slipped inside the "O" and used to exert an outward pressure to force the thumb and index finger apart.

There are many other possible variations, but the essential point is to pit one muscle against another and to determine the correct amount of pressure to apply so that the muscle concerned just stays locked before a test statement is made.

Problems With Muscle Testing:

Most people (80-90%) who are unable to test themselves satisfactorily, will find that they are subconsciously blocking their ability to do it. This will cause a negative test on the statement: "I want to muscle test myself accurately every time I test for anything."

There may be any number of subconscious messages that sabotage their efforts. Such counterproductive behaviour stems from inappropriate or negative belief systems rooted in the subconscious mind. Problems of this sort are called Psychological Reversals, and they result in the subconscious mind overruling the conscious, or logical mind, to the detriment of the individual concerned.

Psychological reversals can cause a wide range of problems in many different areas, and these reversals lie behind many otherwise inexplicable self-defeating actions. Many people make important decisions on the basis of a "gut feeling". When that gut feeling comes from a negatively programmed subconscious, (in other words there is a psychological reversal) the usual result is harmful.

Whatever the reasons behind a psychological reversal, this simply constitutes one more problem, which of course can be treated using BSFF. In the case of muscle testing, just consider the inability to test as a problem, and treat for it accordingly. When this is done, these people will now test positively and should have no further difficulty using muscle testing.

There may be another reason for difficulty which may affect muscle testing in general, and this occurs when the polarity of the body's electromagnetic circuits is switched. This condition is often caused by "neurological disorganisation". Polarity switching is an interesting phenomena in itself, and will be dealt with later. For now, let's just say that it interferes with muscle testing, and must be corrected to get accurate results.

There is a simple test to check for such polarity switching. Have the subject place the palm of one hand squarely on the crown of their head. Now muscle test using their other arm. If they test strong, they are most likely not switched. This may be double-checked by having them turn their hand palm upwards, so that the back of their hand is now resting on the crown of their head. If they now test weak, it confirms that they are not polarity switched.

People who have a polarity switch problem will test weak with the palm down, and strong with the palm up. This condition may be temporarily corrected by gently rubbing on two energy points, located just below the collarbone, about one inch off centre on either side. This can be done while repeating three times: *"I accept myself even though I have this problem"*. These locations are called the K-27 points, and are illustrated in photo number 5.

Photo # 5

Note that this procedure provides a temporary answer only. It is then necessary to go through the BSFF steps (focusing on this problem) to correct this reversal permanently.

Polarity switching may even occur when the subject is facing in a particular direction. Have the subject try an East-West alignment while testing with the palm up and palm down method.

Then try the same test with the subject aligned in a North-South direction. If a switching problem is indicated, use the technique involving the K-27 points to correct it.

Holding something like a plastic kitchen baggy will switch polarity and cause a weak muscle test. Fluorescent lighting, microwaves, home appliances, and metal objects (eyeglasses with metal frames may be a problem here) held near the midpoint of the body may also cause problems. Although it sounds a bit bizarre, recall that electrical signals sent to the muscles are very tiny, so it is not surprising that low-level electromagnetic radiations in our environment may effect muscle testing.

It is widely recognised that switched electromagnetic circuits can contribute to neurological disorganisation, thus interfering with thinking processes. There is also growing evidence that living near high-tension power lines may cause some forms of cancer, possibly by disrupting the body's natural energy field.

Muscle testing may pose a problem in the initial stages, particularly if somebody wants to work alone in the privacy of their own room. Lacking experience, they may not get the results they wish. If this happens, just persevere, and remember, muscle testing is only a means of getting feedback from the subconscious.

It is not the treatment. The BSFF procedure is what does the job, and BSFF doesn't require the fine touch and experience that muscle testing does- it will work regardless.

Nevertheless, anyone can learn to muscle test properly, and the way to do that is to get rid of the obstacles. Nearly everyone who has initial difficulty getting clear muscle testing results will test strongly on these three statements:

"I'm too dumb to learn such a delicate skill."
"I don't deserve such help."
"It's just too weird for me."

If this is the case, then the test statement has revealed a problem, which should be treated as such and removed through BSFF. When that is done, the results should now test weak, and the path is now clear for successful testing.

As with any new skill, the ability to muscle test will improve with experience, and if difficulties are encountered, there is always an answer. For example, even when muscle testing is working well with a client, counselors will sometimes get a weak test on both of two incompatible statements.

When this happens, the answer is to test for this statement: "I don't want to know the answer to this issue." Almost always, the muscle will test strongly on this statement. The answer is to treat this as a problem and clear it up with BSFF. Then retest for this "don't want to know" objection, and you will likely get a clear difference. Once that is cleared up, the original questions can proceed.

The key point is that the subconscious mind has all the information about past experiences and psychological states. It may well act to block some of these details initially, yet they may be accessed through skillful muscle testing.

The statements: "My subconscious mind knows the answer to this question" and "it will tell me the answer" must test affirmative for the information to be obtained. If the second part draws a negative response, treat for it with BSFF.

Remember that test statements must be made as definite assertions, not questions. Use definite statements, as if they are already true, then challenge the statement by muscle testing. To see if a problem is treatable by BSFF in the first place, use the statement: "This problem has emotional roots." If the muscle test is positive, then the problem may be cured by BSFF.

If the problem does not have emotional roots, then it is not treatable by BSFF. It should be noted, though, that even in the case of problems whose solutions lie outside the scope of BSFF, the distress and anxiety generated by the problem may well be alleviated by BSFF.

Possible Objections:

Now that you have read over the first part of this manual and have acquired a basic understanding of BSFF, the logical part of your mind may raise many objections. It is natural to question any new knowledge, and the very simplicity of the method works against embracing it. It just seems too good to be true!

Such scepticism is normal, particularly because so little is actually known about why the method works. When it comes to understanding the complex operations of the brain, contemporary science is still in its infancy. We don't even know where and how memories are stored, for example, despite countless laboratory experiments and the sacrifice of a multitude of test animals in brain experiments.

Here are just a few objections that may stand in the way of giving the method a fair trial:

"I don't have the time to do this"
"My therapist doesn't use BSFF"

"This sounds too strange to take seriously"
"I can't understand this, so I won't use it"
"Everybody will think I'm nuts if I try this"
"It willl be too disappointing if it doesn't work"
"My problem is hopeless. What's the use of trying?"
"Interesting. I'll do something about it later"

As well as the usual healthy scepticism, it should be noted that the conscious mind may well want to torpedo any attempts at mental reform. Entrenched belief systems may be negative, but they may nevertheless fight tooth and nail to maintain the status quo. Don't get derailed or put off. With only a modest investment of time and effort, you could be on your way to a brighter future. There's nothing to lose but your problems!

Whatever objections, logical or otherwise, that may occur, the potential rewards are huge and well worth the effort. Don't let any of these objections stop you. If you still have any doubts about trying BSFF, treat for those doubts and they will melt away. The beauty of the BSFF system is that results can be quick and obvious. Problems can be systematically eliminated, and each objection or problem that is overcome provides the confidence to continue.

Where To Begin:

Once initial objections are overcome and a commitment is made to try the method, what's the best place to start? Many will have had a particular problem in mind when they bought this manual, and if that is the case, the starting point for them may be obvious.

In addition, clearing up one problem may unearth a related concern, and indeed set in train a whole chain reaction of related issues. Each problem overcome will tend to give new insights and point the way to other concerns that should also be addressed.

Some issues though, are so widespread that they may be considered "global" problems. By cutting to the heart of the matter, and treating these first, it may significantly reduce the number of individual things that require attention.

It is very common for people to hold a poor image of themselves, and to lack confidence in their abilities. How common? It is revealing to look at some test questions that Dr. Nims routinely uses with new clients. Let's consider self-image first. Dr. Nims asks the client to repeat the following eight statements, while he muscle tests each response:

"I like myself."
"I'm a good person."
"I have personal value and worth."
"I deserve good things in life."
"I deserve to be loved."
"I deserve God's love."
"I have a good mind."
"I have a good body."

Two observations are in order here. While the question about God's love would be meaningless to an atheist or agnostic, the Christian ethic that makes humility a virtue will also tend to make Christians feel a little guilty if they answer these questions in the affirmative. Perhaps this helps to explain the second point, which is, that a person may believe these statements about themselves to be substantially correct, but at the subconscious level, they believe the exact opposite.

The extent of this tendency is revealed in the fact that over the course of six years doing muscle testing for these statements, Dr. Nims found that among the several hundred people tested, only one person tested positively for all eight statements! Of greater significance is the revealing fact that only rarely does he find a person who tests positively on even one of these statements!

This strongly indicates that a poor self-image is a global problem. Equally disturbing, the vast majority of people also test negatively to the statement "I want to be happy."

How good do people generally feel about their abilities and attributes? To find out, Dr. Nims gets clients to make the following eight statements, while muscle testing for the validity of each:

"I am good at things."
"I am a capable person."
"I can learn most things and do them well."
"I have some good talents, skills and abilities."
"I have a skillful mind."
"I have a skillful body."
"My body is attractive."
"I run my life well."

All of these eight statements refer to the level of our self-confidence, and how our subconscious mind evaluates our skills, talents, abilities and personal attributes. Once again, most people test negatively to all of these statements, which usually comes as a bit of a shock to those tested.

If our own subconscious mind holds such a negative view of us, the only conclusion to be drawn is that it will act to undermine our thoughts, views, feelings and behaviour patterns in myriad ways, which will affect almost every aspect of our lives in harmful ways.

There are too many negatives present in our various cultures. Most of us have been subjected to criticism, name-calling, ridicule, rejection, neglect, shame, embarrassment, scorn, humiliation and other derogatory things by both peers and authority figures.

We have been brainwashed for far too long with the idea that humility is a fit state for man. Better by far to accept Aristotle's concept that a proper sense of self-worth is the virtue midway between the two "sins" of humility at the one extreme, and vanity at the other.

Clearing up the sad state of affairs in ethics and our society is beyond our scope here, but the good news is that BSFF can help clear away much of the damage done by this mental rubbish and allow us to get on with happy, productive lives.

All of these statements that elicit a negative response should be treated as if they are one problem. That is, one sequence of BSFF steps should be used for the self-image problem, and this should be followed up by another BSFF session for the self-confidence problem.

Go through the statements and muscle testing if you have someone to help you, or if you feel confident (there's that word again!) with the self-testing procedure. The short way is that since these problems are so universal, just assume you have them and go ahead and treat for them as a matter of course. Don't forget to treat for being angry with yourself for having these problems, and follow this with the forgiveness treatment sequence.

Once these negatives have been swept away, and replaced with a more positive outlook, it will then be time to address individual problems of a more specific nature.

Constructing Test Statements:

It is important to keep in mind that a positive muscle test means that the statement concerned is 100% true, as far as the person's subconscious mind is concerned, at the time of the test. Conversely, a negative test may still be partially true, or even 95% true. Because of this, there can be a dramatically different response to seemingly minor or innocent changes in wording. Accordingly, it is just as important to know what not to say as it is to know what to include.

Consider the following statements that might be put to someone who has an illness:

"I want to be well."
"I'm willing to be well."
"I'm willing to be well now."
"I will do everything necessary, starting now, to see that I get well quickly."

These are all different statements, and may well test differently. The subconscious mind and its programming is highly precise and literal, indeed, almost computer-like. Anyone who has tried to alter computer programming via typed-in instructions will be well aware that a misplaced punctuation mark spells failure.

The subconscious mind may not be quite that literal, but by using test statements such as those above, Dr. Nims has found that those with a malady will test that they want to keep the condition. Further, and more incredible, testing will show that the subconscious will specify the number of days, hours and minutes that must pass before they will allow themselves to get well! The answer to this one, of course, is to reprogram the subconscious with the appropriate BSFF treatment.

This intriguing characteristic of the subconscious mind extends, of course, into all areas of human endeavor. Thus, muscle testing may reveal that somebody's subconscious will not allow them to earn more than $32,561 per annum, or their golf score is not allowed to break 90, and other such bizarre revelations.

Those who wish to explore such subconsciously-induced limitations should do so by carefully framing their test statements, and then using muscle testing. As to the numbers, it is very similar to a game of 20 questions. In the medical example given, you might start with something like: "I will let myself get well within 20 days." Depending on the response, increase or decrease the number, until you find out just where the subconscious stands on the issue.

Clinicians seeking to discover how many emotional roots are connected to a particular problem might muscle test using the statement: "There are more than 1000 roots to this problem." If the test was positive, they would then use the statement: "There are more than 1500 roots to this problem." If the answer was negative, they would split the difference and test again, until the number was found.

This method may also be used to determine such things as when the first emotional root experience happened, with statements like: "It happened before I was ten years old." If positive, they would test for before five years old, and so forth until the answer was found. This may be narrowed down to the precise month, day, hour and minute that the event occurred, if so desired. Such is the power of the subconscious mind.

 As experience is gained, and the practitioner becomes more skilled at muscle testing, they will likely find that their intuition will develop to the point where less guess work is required, and fewer questions will do the job. Because of its instant feedback, muscle testing is a tremendous way to learn, and get results fast. Find out what is going on at a subconscious level with muscle testing, then fix it with BSFF!

Ethical Considerations:

It must be emphasised that BSFF and muscle testing are not parlour games, or an evening's fun around an ouija board. They are serious therapeutical tools. Anything capable of reprogramming our subconscious minds is to be taken seriously and treated with caution.

There are no hidden dangers to the method, and it is quite safe when used in a responsible manner. Where other people are involved, users of BSFF must ensure they have the full agreement of the other party and should avoid issues that may cause distress or embarrassment.

Counsellors in particular are aware of a client's vulnerability to sensitive issues, and the possibility of legal questions arising through treatment. They are cautious about exploring the possibility of uncovering past abuses and dark secrets. The subconscious may choose to hide many things as a coping technique. Only if the client is completely willing, should a counsellor proceed into these sensitive areas. Such readiness should always be confirmed by muscle testing.

The safest plan of attack for counsellors in such circumstances is to first eliminate the client's distress, then wait for the client to bring up the heavier issues, when and if they are ready. This is good advice for all of us. After all, it is not necessary to dredge up all the roots of a problem, anyway.

BSFF can cut through the Gordion knot faced by conventional therapy techniques. This is the purpose behind statements like: ***"I am eliminating all of the sadness in all of the roots- and the deepest cause- of all of this problem."***

Instant BSFF:

Combinations of problems are called "issues" and will require multiple treatments, one for each problem, until the entire issue is resolved. Even though a single BSFF treatment does not require much time, it may seem a bit lengthy when several related problems must be dealt with in succession.

There is a sort of mental shorthand that may be used once you are familiar with the BSFF procedure. It involves giving a once-only instruction to your subconscious mind. The statement is rather long, because it is meant to be thorough and comprehensive. What it does is allow you to initiate a BSFF treatment at any future time by simply using a cue word or short phrase to trigger the BSFF sequence, without the need to go through the full tapping procedure.

To program your subconscious to activate the BSFF treatment upon receipt of the cue word, carefully give the following instruction to your subconscious mind:

"Whenever I consciously notice any problem that I want to eliminate, whether or not I can identify the problem with words, and I consciously think or speak the cue/trigger word or phrase that I will use, you will do whatever you can to completely and permanently eliminate the problem."

"You will do this from now on, for any problem I notice and want to treat, whenever I initiate a treatment with one of my cues. You will do this for me for any and all cues that I tell you that I will use. I simply need only notice a problem and initiate the treatment with my thought of any of my cues."

Once that is done, cue words may be added at any time by telling your subconscious mind- "I am adding these words as another treatment cue."

There. A bit involved, but once done, your subconscious will implement the BSFF procedure every time you use any of your cue words to initiate treatment.

The cue words you choose to use is a personal decision. Just choose those that have meaning for you. They should be concise, but they may be serious, humorous, whimsical, or whatever you wish.

Once this is set up to work, the beauty of it is that as soon as a problem pops into your awareness, it can be dealt with, on the spot, whether you are at home, at a party, at work or anywhere else. However many people are present, only you will be aware of what you are doing. Much better than letting treatment slip until you can find the time and privacy to deal with it.

It is recommended though, that when time permits, you follow up by using the forgiveness procedure on these problems to specifically deal with any judgmental tendencies, which if left behind, may undo the previous good work.

A Professional Approach:

In planning your own personal BSFF program, it might be helpful to consider how a clinical psychologist proceeds with clients on a first session. After being introduced to BSFF theory, including the definitions of emotional roots and deepest causes, Dr. Nims muscle tests clients for the following statement:

"I can use this simple procedure to eliminate every problem I ever choose to treat."

About half will test negative on this statement, and when this happens, he has the clients rub gently on the K27 spots, as illustrated in photo #5, while repeating three times:

"I accept myself, even though I have this problem." this will correct the reversal temporarily (for about 20-30 minutes).

This allows time to do the BSFF treatment to eliminate this problem on a permanent basis. Subconscious programming that BSFF may not be able to eliminate problems on a reliable basis constitutes a mental block, which of course will have emotional roots and a deepest cause. A BSFF treatment will remove this problem, and muscle testing is then used to confirm that this change has occurred in the subconscious mind. Once corrected, it will not be necessary to ever treat for that problem again.

Next, to reduce the likelihood of global psychological reversals reestablishing themselves later on, Dr. Nims gives the following instruction directly to the client's subconscious mind as part of the first treatment:

"Now, I am saying this to your conscious mind and to your subconscious mind. Whenever you are treating any problem, you are not only eliminating the emotional roots and the deepest cause (belief system), but, you are also eliminating anything that would make you keep the problem, ever take it back, ever permit it to come back, ever passively allow it to come back, ever accept it back, or ever be receptive to it coming back."

He uses this instruction only once, preceding the first treatment with each client, and muscle tests to ensure the subconscious has accepted this instruction. Interestingly, he reports that muscle testing invariably confirms that the subconscious agrees to incorporate and utilise all that it has learned about BSFF into every treatment.

Dr. Nims himself expresses his surprise at the universal acceptance of subconscious minds to categorically implement such seemingly complex processes without hesitation, and to do so in a creative, skillful and reliable manner.

The message is that the subconscious mind is not something that tries to hold you back. It may have been negatively programmed, and that programming is holding you back, but the subconscious is merely a neutral party obeying your instructions. It is just as happy to accept a new, positive set of instructions and apply them with the same zeal as it did with the previous negative ones.

Following this initial setup procedure to deal with psychological reversals which might otherwise cause recurring problems, Dr. Nims then goes on to treat other problems in succession until the client reports that he or she is clear of all problems in the identified area of concern, and muscle testing is used to confirm that this is so.

The Apex Problem:

Precisely because BSFF is such a fast, effective treatment, it can be difficult for the client involved to accept that the problems of a lifetime can be swept away in the space of a few minutes. Indeed, this can initiate a process of denial, in which it is held that the problem never existed in the first place.

When treating clients with TFT (though field therapy), Dr. Roger Callahan noted a response which he dubbed "The Apex Problem." This was the tendency for a client to accurately report the expected and predicted improvement, but then refusing to credit the treatment for bringing it about!

In such cases, the client has difficulty believing that the changes are due to the therapy, even though the express purpose of the therapy was to bring about those very changes! Note that the person is not trying to minimise or distort the changes, they simply can't associate it with the therapy. Instead, they will compulsively offer an alternative explanation for the improvement which makes sense to them. They rationalise the change.

In some cases, clients will rewrite their history after treatment, effectively forgetting that they ever had a problem in the first place. This is not a case of ingratitude, but rather an inability to absorb the mental shock. With the sudden erasure of old, negative value sets, comes the necessary reordering of much information, and perhaps the discarding of many cherished opinions.

This phenomena is also common among clients treated with BSFF. Yet, while the conscious mind may go into denial mode, the subconscious has a complete and detailed account of the person's history. If any change has taken place, it will know what that change was and precisely when it happened. Since muscle testing allows us to access the subconscious mind, it follows that testing will allow the client to perceive the significance of pre and post testing, and thereby to understand that something quite profound has occurred.

A test statement can be constructed to show what the state of affairs was at any particular time. Thus the therapist can say, "We are testing for five minutes ago." or "We are testing for just before we treated this problem." This allows a before and after comparison, which will show whether the problem was there at any particular time. When a present time muscle test is done, backing up the removal of the problem, the significance is borne home to the client.

Such direct physical evidence from their own bodies can also make the transition to their new mental state easier, by alleviating any feelings of guilt or shame. It helps them to realise that their motivations weren't so bad after all, when they understand that they acted as they did because they were programmed that way, before they could do anything about it.

The Temporal Tap:

There is another very useful tool for programming the subconscious mind, which accomplishes similar results to hypnosis, without requiring the trance state to be effective. This method is ideally suited to inject positive affirmations directly into the subconscious mind.

In essence, the technique consists of first choosing an affirmation that you wish to become true and operative in your life. This affirmation is then repeated once for each of three tapping sequences, involving the "Temporal-Sphenoidal Line," which is composed of twenty energy points under the scalp, on either side of the head, around the ears.

Tapping on these energy points acts to bypass the conscious mind, so that the subconscious mind receives, and instantly acts upon, whatever suggestion is being presented to it at that time.

The tapping is done by using all of the fingers and the thumb tip of each hand together, and the tapping proceeds in a circular motion, starting just forward of the ear canal, and then proceeding up and around the outside edge of the ear until you reach the back center of the ear, just opposite the starting point. This is done on both sides of the head simultaneously, and follows the location of the T-S line.

While tapping in a firm manner, the affirmation may be either said out loud or simply repeated mentally. This tapping, and the accompanying statement, is done three times in succession. You should then wait for about half an hour before repeating any specific affirmation. In the meantime, you may repeat the process with other affirmations, moving smoothly from one set of three sequences for each affirmation, to as many other affirmations as you choose.

Repeating the affirmation and tapping sequence several times a day can speed up the process of instilling a new message into the subconscious mind. To confirm that this has been done, muscle test with a statement such as: "I now believe, accept, and live out this affirmation in, and for myself continually."

Again, other similar statements may be used if you feel more comfortable with a different phrase. Just bear in mind that the subconscious is very literal, precise and specific, and will respond in accordance with exactly what the words mean to it- not how others may interpret them.

It is recommended that you do not take on too many affirmations at any one time, since affirmations should be repeated several times a day. It is the nature of the instillation process that they need reinforcement to be fully integrated into the subconscious mind.

Of course, once muscle testing confirms that a specific affirmation is in place, you may move on to others. Because of this repetition, it is a good idea to write down your affirmations to prevent inadvertent word changes.

The temporal tapping process will also work best if you first use BSFF to eliminate any competing problems from the subconscious. In short, the more your subconscious mind is cleared of competing programming, the faster the new programming will be instilled and operative.

Constructing Your Affirmations:

The basic procedure is pretty simple- merely tapping around the upper periphery of each ear, while repeating the affirmation three times. The real skill in this technique lies in composing your affirmations, so a few words on this subject are in order at this point.

Affirmations are constructed as definite statements, in present time, as if the statement were already completely true. Leave it to the subconscious mind to make the internal and external adjustments required to make the statement true for you.

Make affirmations concise, yet comprehensive and inclusive. They may be any positive thinking statements in any area that you feel is required- mental, emotional, occupational, financial, social or whatever other areas you can think of, that are important for you.

Possibilities for constructive affirmations appear to be endless, and may be adapted to whatever positive change you would like to see in your life. There may be specific ones of interest to you that will be obvious, but just to close off this section, consider the following global statements that you may wish to use, or adapt for your purposes:

"I trust myself to make wise decisions and choices about everything."

"I always do everything necessary to establish and maintain excellent mental, physical and emotional health."

"I permit myself to be happy and contented with my life."

"I choose to be happy and contented in all circumstances, no matter what is going on around me."

"I am skillful, alert and focused in all of my activities."

And how about this affirmation to end with:

"I carry out my plans quickly, without procrastination."

****

www.ingramcontent.com/pod-product-compliance
Lightning Source LLC
Chambersburg PA
CBHW050845290526
45792CB00002B/527